Material Matters

Chemical Reactions

Carol Baldwin

Raintree

Chicago, Illinois

For information, address the publisher:
Raintree, 100 N. LaSalle, Suite 1200, Chicago, IL 60602

Printed and bound in China
08 07 06 05 04
10 9 8 7 6 5 4 3 2 1

Library of Congress Cataloging-in-Publication Data
Baldwin, Carol.
  Chemical reactions / Carol Baldwin.
     p. cm. -- (Material matters)
Includes bibliographical references and index.
Contents: Matter -- Describing matter -- Changing matter -- Describing chemical reactions -- Kinds of chemical reactions -- Chemical reactions and energy -- Reaction rates -- Some chemical reactions -- Chemical reactions in nature.
  ISBN 1-4109-0549-7 (lib. bdg.), 1-4109-0936-0 (Pbk.)
  1. Chemical reactions--Juvenile literature. 2. Strength of materials--Juvenile literature. [1. Chemical reactions. 2. Strength of materials.] I. Title. II. Series: Baldwin, Carol, 1943-   Material matters.
  QD501.B234 2004
  541.3'9--dc21
                          2003010110

Acknowledgments
The publisher would like to thank the following for permission to reproduce photographs:
Pp. 4, 20, 35, 41 Tudor Photography; pp. 4–5, 8, 15, 25, 36–37; 40 (left) Corbis; pp. 5 (top), 18–19 Kennedy Space Center/NASA; pp. 5 (middle), 36, 45 Geophotos/T. Waltham; pp. 5 (bottom) 42–43 Forensic Alliance; p. 6 Robert Harding; pp. 6–7, 7 Photodisc; p. 9 (left) Alex Bartel/Science Photo Library; pp. 9 (right), 14, 38 Art Directors & Trip; p.10 R. Krist/Corbis; pp. 10–11 C. O'Rear/Corbis; p. 11 T. Lang/Corbis; p. 12 Foodpix; pp. 12–13 O. Franken/Corbis; p.13 Chris Honeywell; pp. 14–15 L. Lewis/FLPA; p. 16 Duomo/Corbis; pp. 16–17 P. Scoones/Science Photo Library; p. 17 C. Smedley/Art Directors & Trip; p. 18 Digital Vision; p. 19 W. Meinderts/FLPA; pp. 20–21 R.Tidman/FLPA; p. 21 CNRI/Science Photo Library; p. 22 G. Rowell/Corbis; pp. 22–23 P. Turnley/Corbis; p. 23 MacFadden Publishing/Corbis; pp. 24(right), 32 Associated Press; p. 24 (left) M. Chillmaid/Science Photo Library; p. 26 D. Parker/Science Photo Library; pp. 26–27 D. Spears/Science Photo Library; p. 27 Trevor Clifford; p. 28 E. Whiting Corbis; pp. 28–29 R. Gehman/Corbis; p. 29 Jet Propulsion Laboratory/NASA; p. 30, 30–31 Charles D. Winters/Science Photo Library; p. 31 C. Kapolka/Art Directors & Trip; p. 33 (right) Andrew Lambert; pp. 33 (left), 44 Mark Perry/Simon Peachey/TDG Nexus; p. 34 P. Ryan/Scripps/Science Photo Library; pp. 34–35 Gerard Lacz/FLPA; p. 37 Australia Picture Library/Art Directors & Trip; pp. 38–39 Michael Abbey/Science Photo Library; p. 39 Gareth Boden; p. 40 (right) T. Freeman/Art Directors & Trip; p. 42 A. Lambert/Art Directors & Trip; p. 43 T. Stewart/Corbis.
Cover photograph of a reaction taking place in a test tube reproduced with permission of Lester Lefkowitz/Corbis.

Every effort has been made to contact copyright holders of any material reproduced in this book.
Any omissions will be rectified in subsequent printings if notice is given to the publishers.
Disclaimer
All the Internet addresses (URLs) given in this book were valid at the time of going to press. However, due to the dynamic nature of the Internet, some addresses may have changed, or sites may have changed or ceased to exist since publication. While the author and publishers regret any inconvenience this may cause readers, nor esponsibility for any such changes can be accepted by either the author or the publishers.

Contents

Some words are shown in bold, **like this.** You can find out what they mean by looking in the glossary. You can also look out for them in the Word Bank at the bottom of each page.

Explosion!

Different colors

Different chemicals in fireworks shoot out sparks in different colors. Chemicals that contain sodium produce yellow sparks. Chemicals that contain strontium produce red sparks. A bright, white color usually comes from magnesium. And chemicals that contain copper or barium produce green sparks.

A firework shell shoots high into the air like a rocket. Boom! The shell explodes. A spectacular splash of red spreads across the sky. A few seconds later another firework explodes. A huge ball of brilliant white sparks lights up the sky. Next comes a firework that explodes in two stages. First there are sizzling, spinning wheels of green, then a whistling sound as a burst of yellow explodes outward. Lights, colors, and sounds are all part of firework displays. They show that some sort of change is taking place in the materials that make up the fireworks.

Fireworks are dangerous because they contain explosive chemicals.

Word Bank   chemical reaction   change that produces one or more new substances

Changes all around us

Materials around us change all the time. Some changes happen naturally. Others are caused by people. Some changes, like the explosion of fireworks, take less than a second. Other changes take longer, such as wood burning and leaving ashes behind. Some changes, like the rusting of a car, may take years. When people dye cloth, fry an egg, or bake a loaf of bread, they are changing those materials. Changes also happen inside us. When we grow, eat food, and even think, changes are happening in the materials that make up our bodies. To understand what happens when materials change, you need to know something about **chemical reactions.**

The lights and noise of fireworks are used in celebrations around the world.

Find out later . . .

What kind of chemical reaction powers the space shuttle?

How do caves form?

How do police use chemical reactions?

Matter

You need to know something about **matter** in order to understand how materials change. Everything around us is made of matter. The food we eat, the clothes we wear, and the buildings we live in are matter. All matter is made of tiny **particles** called **atoms.** But not all atoms are alike. The atoms in a pencil point are different from the atoms in water.

Elements

There are about a hundred different kinds of atom. Each kind of atom is a different **element.** Silver, hydrogen, carbon, and oxygen are elements. Each element is made of only one kind of atom. Elements cannot be broken down into simpler substances.

What is matter?

A light bulb is matter. But the light it produces is not matter. Neither is the heat given off by a light bulb. The light and heat are forms of **energy.** Electricity is a form of energy that powers the light bulb. A lightning flash is electrical energy, and the crash of thunder is sound energy.

Fast Fact

Atoms are made up of even smaller particles called protons, neutrons, and electrons. The atoms in different elements have different numbers of protons.

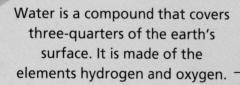

Water is a compound that covers three-quarters of the earth's surface. It is made of the elements hydrogen and oxygen. ⟶

Word Bank   atom   smallest particle of an element
compound   substance made of two or more elements joined together

Compounds

Compounds are substances that are made of atoms of more than one element. In a compound the atoms of elements join in special ways that hold them tightly together. Compounds can be broken down into simpler substances. But it is often difficult to separate the atoms of a compound. Table salt is a compound made of two elements, sodium, and chlorine. Sugar is a compound made of carbon, hydrogen, and oxygen. Carbon dioxide is made of carbon and oxygen. A compound always has a set number of each kind of atom that makes it up. For example, **molecules** of water are made of two atoms of hydrogen joined with one atom of oxygen.

Mixtures

Mixtures are materials made of two or more elements or compounds that are not joined. Mixtures do not contain a set amount of the different substances that make them up.

Fast Fact
A compound of another element with oxygen is called an **oxide**.

Pizza is a mixture of different amounts of sauce, cheese, and other toppings.

element   substance made of only one kind of atom
matter   anything that takes up space and has mass

Finding the right car

People use the physical properties of parked vehicles to help them find their car in a parking lot. They may first search by size and shape and then by color. Finally, they might look at all the cars of the right color until they find the right make and model.

Matter can be described in two main ways. It has different features called **properties**. Matter can have different **physical properties** and different **chemical properties**.

Physical properties

Physical properties include color, shape, hardness, taste, smell, and **state of matter**. Another physical property is whether heat or electricity can travel through the matter. You can find out the physical properties of something without changing it.

An onion has a strong smell and a strong taste. It is also round and solid. When you describe an onion, you are saying what its physical properties are. Some physical properties of lemon juice are its yellow color, its liquid state, and its sour taste.

The physical properties of cars include size, shape, and color.

Word Bank   chemical property   feature that tells how a substance will react

Chemical properties

The **chemical properties** of a substance tell us how it will act in the presence of other substances. Wood has the chemical property of being able to burn in air. We make use of this chemical property when we burn wood in a fireplace.

If we leave a bicycle or garden tool outdoors for a long time, it may rust. Rust forms when oxygen in the air joins with iron. The fact that iron can rust is one of its chemical properties. The fact that milk will turn sour if left sitting on the kitchen counter is a chemical property. You can only find out the chemical properties of something when it changes.

Iron is a solid, hard metal. Iron can be separated from other nonmagnetic materials because it has the physical property of being attracted by a magnet.

Colored bottles

Vitamins usually do not come in clear plastic bottles. Most come in bottles that do not let light in. Many vitamins have the chemical property of changing when light strikes them.

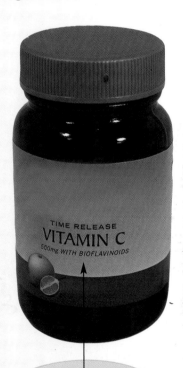

TIME RELEASE
VITAMIN C
500mg WITH BIOFLAVINOIDS

Dark bottles protect vitamins and keep them from changing.

physical property   feature that can be seen or measured without changing what a substance is made of

Changing Matter

The Liberty Bell

The Liberty Bell was made in London by pouring melted bronze metal into a mold. Once poured, a large bell must cool very slowly to prevent the metal from cracking as it changes back to a solid.

The Liberty Bell cracked and had to be recast twice before it was hung in Philadelphia. It has not been rung since 1846.

Physical changes

An artist might carve a sculpture from a piece of wood. As he carves the wood, he changes its shape. The changes he makes do not change the wood into something else. The wood is still wood. Changes in the way something looks, but not in what makes it up, are **physical changes**.

A change in size is also a physical change. A rubber band can stretch and change its size. But it has not changed into something different. Matter can also change from solid to liquid, liquid to gas, and back again. When something changes its **state of matter** like this, it is a physical change. When water changes to ice in a freezer, it is still water.

When this melted copper cools, it will turn back to a solid. But what makes up the metal does not change. So it is a physical change.

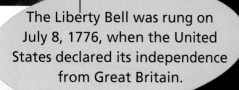

The Liberty Bell was rung on July 8, 1776, when the United States declared its independence from Great Britain.

Word Bank   odorless   having no smell
physical change   change in how something looks, but not in what makes it up

Chemical changes

When wood burns in a fireplace, what is left is not wood. The wood joins with oxygen in the air and changes to something else. The burning of wood is a chemical change or **chemical reaction.** A chemical reaction is a change in which new substances are formed. When wood burns, the new substances are ashes, **water vapor,** and carbon dioxide gas. The ash formed is a soft, gray powder. The water vapor and carbon dioxide are colorless, **odorless** gases. The new substances formed in a chemical reaction look different and act differently from the wood.

The wood and oxygen are called the **reactants** because they react with each other. The ash and gases are called the **products** because they are produced by the reaction.

Flashlight batteries

Some batteries contain powdered zinc and manganese oxide. The chemical reaction changes the zinc to zinc oxide. It also changes the manganese oxide to manganese. These chemical changes cause electricity to flow to the light bulb, giving off light.

When a flashlight is turned on, a chemical change inside the battery makes electricity.

product   substance formed by a chemical reaction
reactant   substance that reacts with another substance during a chemical reaction

11

Cooking pancakes

The holes you see inside pancakes are clues that a chemical change happened as they cooked. Ingredients in the recipe react together to make carbon dioxide gas. As the pancake cooks, bubbles of carbon dioxide rise through the batter and pop at its surface.

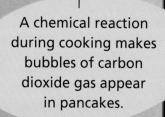

A chemical reaction during cooking makes bubbles of carbon dioxide gas appear in pancakes.

Clues to chemical changes

You can be sure a **chemical reaction** is taking place if you see a fire. Fires give off heat, light, and smoke. Some other chemical changes give off heat or light without fire. Giving off **energy** as light, heat, sound, or electricity is a sign of a chemical change.

Sometimes a gas is formed during a chemical reaction. When sodium bicarbonate is placed in vinegar, bubbles of gas form. A color change is another clue that a chemical reaction may have taken place. When sugar is heated for a long time, it will change first to a brown liquid, then to a black solid. Sometimes two clear liquids will form a solid when they are put together. This solid, called a **precipitate**, will make the reaction **mixture** cloudy. Finally, the precipitate will settle to the bottom of the container.

Burning wood gets lighter because the gases produced during burning escape into the air. If we could capture the gases and add their mass to the mass of the ashes, the total would be the same as the original mass of the wood.

Word Bank   mass   amount of matter in an object. It is measured in ounces or pounds (grams or kilograms).

Conservation of mass

During a chemical reaction, new substances are formed. But the amount of **matter,** or **mass,** is the same before and after the reaction takes place. The number of each kind of **atom** does not change. The atoms simply rearrange themselves.

In chemical reactions, no matter is lost and none is made. The mass of the **reactants** equals the mass of the **products.** This statement is called the law of conservation of mass. When iron rusts, it combines with oxygen to form iron oxide. The mass of the iron oxide is equal to the mass of the iron plus the mass of the oxygen. No mass is lost or gained in the reaction.

Burning candles

A candle looks as if it loses mass as it burns. But if you could trap and measure the gases it gives off during burning, you would find that the mass of the candle stub plus the gases equals the mass of the original candle.

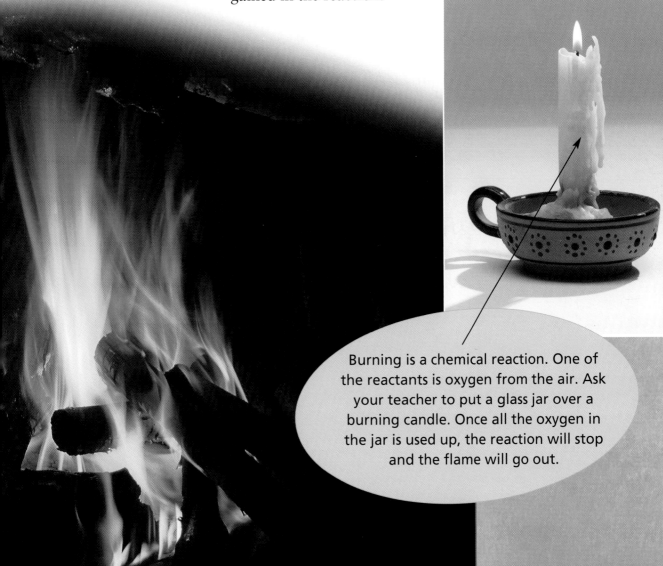

Burning is a chemical reaction. One of the reactants is oxygen from the air. Ask your teacher to put a glass jar over a burning candle. Once all the oxygen in the jar is used up, the reaction will stop and the flame will go out.

precipitate   solid compound, produced in a chemical reaction, that does not dissolve

Kitchen reaction

When you add vinegar to bicarbonate of soda, a chemical reaction happens. The mixed chemicals bubble and foam up inside the container. The vinegar and bicarbonate of soda are the reactants. The bubbles are carbon dioxide gas. But there are two other products, which are shown in the word equation for the reaction.

The equation for this reaction is vinegar + bicarbonate of soda → carbon dioxide + water + sodium ethanoate

Describing chemical reactions

Word equations are one way of describing what happens in a **chemical reaction.** A word equation gives the names of the **reactants** on the left and the names of the **products** on the right. These names are separated by an arrow. The arrow points from the reactants to the products and means "produces."

Water forms as hydrogen reacts with oxygen. The word equation for the formation of water is:

$$\text{hydrogen} + \text{oxygen} \rightarrow \text{water}$$

Silver **tarnishes** when it reacts with tiny amounts of hydrogen sulfide gas in the air. The word equation for the reaction is:

$$\text{silver} + \text{hydrogen sulfide} \rightarrow \text{silver sulfide} + \text{hydrogen}$$

Silver sulfide is the product that forms a dark coating on silver.

Fast Fact
Equations for chemical reactions do not use the = sign like math equations. Instead they use an arrow.

The reaction between copper, carbon dioxide, and **water vapor** in the air forms a layer of green copper carbonate on this copper statue.

Chemical symbols

Chemical symbols are a short way of writing the names of elements. Symbols are either one or two letters. The first is always a capital letter. The second letter is always lower case. Some symbols, like those for hydrogen and oxygen, are the first letter of the element's name. Other symbols, like those for aluminum and calcium, are the first two letters of the element's name. Other elements have two-letter symbols that come from their names but are not the first two letters. The symbol for chlorine, Cl, is an example. Some of these symbols come from the element's name in another language. For example, the symbol for silver, Ag, comes from its Latin name, *argentum*.

Some common chemical symbols

- Oxygen   O
- Hydrogen   H
- Gold   Au
- Sulfur   S
- Chlorine   Cl
- Sodium   Na
- Carbon   C
- Iron   Fe
- Copper   Cu

Fast Fact
The chemical symbol for the metal element tungsten is W. The symbol comes from the metal's German name, *wolfram*.

Sodium and chlorine are both dangerous elements. But they join to form table salt, a very safe compound.

tarnish   to become dull by a reaction with air

Chemical formulas

Chemical symbols can be used to write **formulas.** A formula is a simple way of showing which **atoms** are joined. A formula also shows how many atoms of each **element** are joined together. Air contains oxygen, which has the symbol O_2. The O stands for oxygen. The "2" tells us that two atoms of oxygen are joined. Numbers in chemical formulas are written below the line if they refer to joined atoms. They are written on the line if they refer to atoms or molecules that are not joined. So 2C means two atoms of carbon that are not joined.

Formulas are also used to write the names of **compounds.** If only one atom of an element is part of a compound, there is no number after the symbol. For example, the formula for carbon dioxide is CO_2. The compound carbon dioxide has one atom of carbon and two atoms of oxygen.

Symbol equations

Symbol equations are similar to word equations. But instead of words, they use chemical symbols, formulas, numbers, and an arrow. Words and formulas should not be mixed in a single equation.

The symbol equation for the reaction between hydrogen and oxygen is:

$$2H_2 + O_2 \rightarrow 2H_2O$$

Chlorine

Chlorine can be made from the reaction of manganese oxide and hydrochloric acid. The **products** are manganese chloride, chlorine, and water. The symbol equation for the reaction is:

$$MnO_2 + 4HCl \rightarrow MnCl_2 + Cl_2 + 2H_2O$$

Chlorine is added to swimming pools to kill **bacteria** in the water.

bacteria   living things so small they can only be seen with a microscope
formula   symbols and numbers used to show how atoms are joined

The H_2 and O_2 tell you that both gases are made of two atoms joined together. The large 2 in front of the H_2 tells you that two of these pairs of hydrogen atoms react with one pair of oxygen atoms. The formula for water is H_2O. The large 2 in front of the formula tells you how much water is produced by each set of **reactants.** Notice that on the left side of the arrow there are 4 atoms of hydrogen and 2 atoms of oxygen. On the right side, there are the same number of each kind of atom. This tells you that atoms are not lost or gained during a reaction. They are just rearranged.

Aluminum is used for many things, from food wrappers to airplane wings.

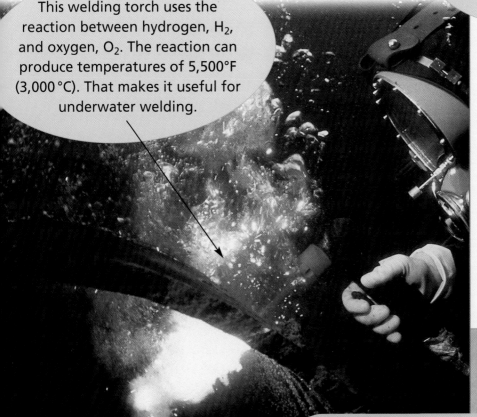

This welding torch uses the reaction between hydrogen, H_2, and oxygen, O_2. The reaction can produce temperatures of 5,500°F (3,000 °C). That makes it useful for underwater welding.

Aluminum

Much aluminum is made from aluminum oxide. The aluminum oxide is melted and electricity is passed through it. This reaction produces aluminum and oxygen. The symbol equation is:

$$2Al_2O_3 \rightarrow 4Al + 3O_2$$

◄◄◄◄◄◄◄◄◄◄◄◄◄◄
Turn back to page 14 to see the word equation for the reaction between hydrogen and oxygen.

symbol equation   way of describing a chemical reaction using chemical formulas

Kinds of Chemical Reactions

Acid in the air

Sulfur oxides from coal-burning power plants can join with water in the air. This reaction produces acids. Nitrogen oxides from car exhausts can also react with water in air. This produces different acids. These acids fall to the earth as **acid rain** or snow.

Synthesis reactions

The word synthesis means "putting together." A **synthesis reaction** happens when two or more **elements** or **compounds** join to form a new compound. For example, iron and sulfur join to form the compound iron sulfide, as shown below. In all synthesis reactions there is only one **product**.

The elements hydrogen and oxygen join to form the compound water. This is a synthesis reaction. Another example of this type of reaction is when the elements carbon and oxygen join to form the compound carbon dioxide.

The compounds calcium oxide and carbon dioxide join in a synthesis reaction to form a new compound, calcium carbonate. This is used to ease upset stomachs because it reacts with excess stomach **acid**.

Decomposition reactions

The word decompose means "break apart." So **decomposition reactions** happen when a compound breaks apart into simpler substances. Decomposition reactions are the opposite of synthesis reactions. In some decomposition reactions, a compound breaks apart to form two elements. This happens when water is split apart to form hydrogen and oxygen.

Acid rain flows into streams or ponds where it can kill plants, frogs, fish, and other life.

decomposition reaction   chemical change in which a compound breaks apart into simpler substances

In other decomposition reactions, one compound breaks apart to form two different compounds. When copper carbonate is heated, it breaks apart to form the compounds copper oxide and carbon dioxide, as shown below. In all decomposition reactions there is only one reactant.

Cu C O O O ⟶ Cu O + C O O

Decomposers

Some living things, such as molds and mushrooms, are called decomposers. They break apart, or decompose, the compounds in dead plants, animals, and waste. Without decomposers, the earth would be covered with this dead **matter.**

Decomposers such as this beefsteak fungus get energy by breaking down compounds in plant waste.

The synthesis reaction between hydrogen and oxygen powers the liftoff of the space shuttle.

synthesis reaction   chemical change in which two or more elements or compounds join to form one compound

Button batteries

Button batteries are used in watches and hearing aids. These batteries use a displacement reaction to produce **energy**. The batteries contain zinc and mercury oxide. During the reaction, zinc displaces the mercury. The products of the reaction are zinc oxide and mercury.

Displacement reactions

In **displacement reactions**, one **element** displaces another element in a **compound**. The **reactants** in a simple displacement reaction are an element and a compound. The **products** are a different element and a different compound.

This kind of reaction is used to extract many metals that are important for industry. Much of the iron we use comes from the compound iron oxide. Ironworkers use carbon to separate iron from iron oxide. The reaction produces iron and carbon dioxide. The carbon takes the place of iron in the **oxide** compound, as shown below. We also extract the metals lead, copper, aluminum, and zinc from their oxides using displacement reactions.

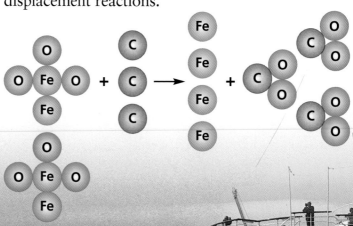

Some ships that sail in the ocean have magnesium bars welded onto their iron hulls. The magnesium is more reactive and displaces iron from any iron compounds that are formed. Rust is a compound of iron. So the magnesium prevents the iron hull of the ship from **corroding** in the saltwater.

corrode   to be damaged by a chemical reaction
displace   to take the place of

Other displacement reactions

In more complex displacement reactions, elements from two different compounds switch places. The reactants are two compounds. The products are also two compounds.

The reaction of silver nitrate with sodium chloride is an example of this kind of displacement reaction. First, both of the compounds are **dissolved** in water. Then one is poured into the other. One of the products is a white solid that appears in the water. This is a **precipitate.** A precipitate is a compound that will not dissolve in water. The precipitate in this reaction is silver chloride. The other product is sodium nitrate. It stays dissolved in the water so you cannot see it. This reaction is shown below.

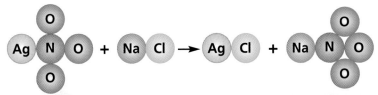

Fast Fact

In this type of displacement reaction, the compounds are like two pairs of dancers that switch partners.

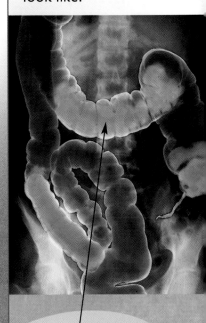

Barium sulfate shows up in X-rays.

displacement reaction   chemical reaction in which one or more elements in a compound displace another element

Reactions and Energy

Rusting

Some chemical reactions are fast, while others are slow. Rusting is an exothermic reaction. But a rusting car does not feel hot to the touch. This is because rusting is a very slow reaction. Rusting metal gives off heat so slowly that it is not noticeable.

Exothermic reactions

When people go camping they often light a campfire to stay warm. Wood gives off heat **energy** when it burns. That heat keeps the campers warm. Wood also gives off light energy when it burns. Any **chemical reaction** that gives off energy is called an **exothermic reaction.** When something burns, it gives off heat and light energy. So burning is an exothermic reaction.

There are many exothermic reactions in which energy is given off more slowly. A **compost** heap containing grass clippings, leaves, and soil slowly warms up. This is because energy is given off as the plants rot. Wet concrete warms up in the reaction that makes it harden. The heat is a sign that energy is being given off.

▷▷▷▷▷▷▷▷▷▷▷▷
Turn to pages 40–41 to read about other exothermic reactions.

Iron rusts when it reacts with water and oxygen in the air. The brownish-orange compound iron oxide is a product.

Firefighters must deal with tremendous heat given off in a building fire. It can get so hot that steel beams will melt.

Word Bank   electrolysis   using electricity to break a compound apart
endothermic reaction   reaction that needs energy to occur

Endothermic reactions

Some chemical reactions need energy to be added all the time or they will stop. Vegetables will cook as long as they get energy from hot water. If the vegetables are taken out of the hot water and placed in cold water, they stop cooking right away. Any chemical reaction that needs energy to be added all the time is called an **endothermic reaction.**

Water can be separated into hydrogen and oxygen. But the reaction only continues as long as energy in the form of electricity is passed through the water. The process of separating a **compound** using electricity is called **electrolysis.** Electrolysis is used to separate aluminum metal from aluminum oxide. This is also an endothermic reaction.

In the limelight

When limestone is heated, it produces carbon dioxide and calcium oxide (**lime**). When lime is heated to a high temperature, it gives off a bright bluish-white light. This light was used in the early 1800s to light theater stages. This is where the term "in the limelight" came from.

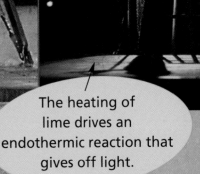

The heating of lime drives an endothermic reaction that gives off light.

Reaction Rates

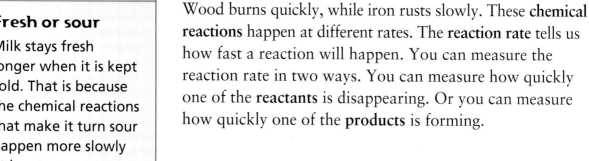

Fresh or sour

Milk stays fresh longer when it is kept cold. That is because the chemical reactions that make it turn sour happen more slowly at low temperatures.

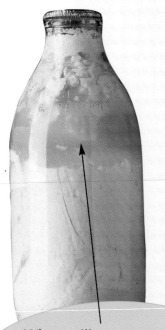

Wood burns quickly, while iron rusts slowly. These **chemical reactions** happen at different rates. The **reaction rate** tells us how fast a reaction will happen. You can measure the reaction rate in two ways. You can measure how quickly one of the **reactants** is disappearing. Or you can measure how quickly one of the **products** is forming.

Temperature

Most chemical reactions speed up when the temperature increases. The high temperature inside an oven speeds up chemical reactions that turn cake batter into a cake. Lowering the temperature slows down most reactions. If you set the oven temperature too low, a cake will not bake properly. Keeping foods cold in a refrigerator slows down the reactions that make food go bad.

When milk turns sour, it separates into a liquid called whey and fatty solids known as curds.

Tiny grain-dust particles contain high amounts of carbon. Their high surface area means that they burn fast enough to cause explosions. This is a danger in places where grain is stored.

Word Bank   concentration   amount of a substance in a certain volume
particle   tiny piece

Concentration

The amount of a substance in a certain amount of space is called the **concentration.** If you increase the concentration, you increase the number of **particles** of a substance in that space. Particles of reactants are more likely to bump into one another and react when their concentrations are high. So a high concentration of reactant will speed up a reaction.

Particle size

The size of reactant particles also affects how fast a reaction will happen. You can start a campfire more easily with small twigs than with big logs. The smaller reactant particles are, the bigger **surface area** of reactant there is. That means more of the particles will touch each other and react. This makes the reaction faster.

Flaming Flour

Any **compound** that contains carbon and hydrogen and has tiny particles can explode. Flour particles are so tiny that they have a huge surface area and burn rapidly and easily. As one particle burns, it lights all the other particles near it.

Flames can flash through a cloud of flour in an explosion. In 1965 an explosion at this London flour mill killed four people.

reaction rate   measure of how fast a chemical reaction happens
surface area   parts of a substance in contact with another reactant

Catalysts

Sometimes **chemical reactions** are too slow to be useful. People use **catalysts** to speed up reactions. A catalyst speeds up a chemical reaction but it does not take part in the reaction. So the catalyst does not change or get used up. You end up with the same amount of catalyst you started with.

Catalysts are used to remove pollution fom the exhaust fumes of cars and trucks. The exhaust gases pass through a catalytic converter, which is filled with small beads coated with metal. The coating speeds up reactions that convert harmful exhaust gases into less dangerous substances that do not **pollute** the air as much. The large surface area means that the maximum amount of gases come into contact with the catalysts.

➤ ➤ ➤ ➤ ➤ ➤ ➤ ➤ ➤ ➤ ➤ ➤

Turn to page 43 to find out how a catalyst helps police solve crimes.

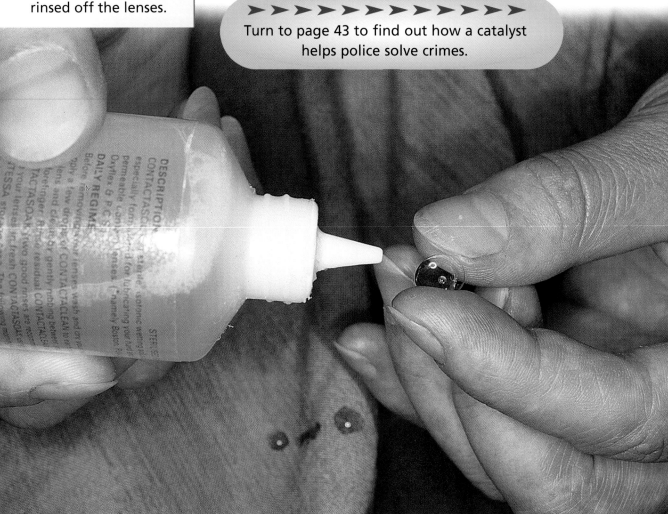

catalyst   substance that speeds up a reaction without being changed
enzyme   chemical that speeds up reactions in living things

Enzymes are catalysts that speed up reactions inside and outside the bodies of living things. All living things use enzymes. When a spider bites an insect, it pours enzymes into the insect's body. The enzymes catalyze digestion of the insect's body and turn it into a soft goo. Then the spider sucks up the resulting food. Plants turn the **energy** of sunlight into food in the form of sugar. Enzymes control the chemical reactions that trap sunlight and break water apart so plants can make their own food.

Inhibitors

Sometimes reactions happen too quickly. Foods and medicines can spoil too quickly because of chemical reactions. People use **inhibitors** to slow down these chemical reactions. Many cereal boxes contain a **compound** called BHT. The BHT in the packaging material slows down the chemical reactions that make the cereal get stale.

Keeping chopped apples cold will also slow down the chemical reaction that turns them brown.

Some spiders digest their prey before they eat it. They inject enzymes that catalyze the breakdown of the victim's body.

Browning apples

Pieces of peeled, raw apple will react with oxygen in the air, producing a brown substance. Adding lemon juice to apples as soon as they are cut greatly slows down the reaction. That is because **acids** in the lemon juice act as inhibitors.

inhibitor   substance that slows down a chemical reaction
pollute   add harmful substances to air, water, or land

Some Chemical Reactions

Burning without enough oxygen

Each year carbon monoxide kills hundreds of people. Carbon monoxide is a deadly, colorless, **odorless** gas. Burning **fuels** usually produces carbon dioxide. But when there is not enough oxygen the reaction forms carbon monoxide instead. Carbon monoxide detectors sound a loud alarm to warn people of danger in their home.

Oxidation

The reaction of a substance with oxygen is called **oxidation.** Sometimes oxidation happens very quickly. Other times it happens very slowly.

Fast reactions with oxygen

When a substance reacts with oxygen quickly, it is called burning, or **combustion.** A piece of paper, a candle, and a log will all burn. Heat and light **energy** are given off during combustion. This is why combustion is useful. We use combustion to heat our homes and businesses and to run our cars, trucks, and buses.

Combustion can also be harmful. Buildings catch fire and burn. Sometimes people die in fires. Forest fires kill plants and animals and destroy their habitats.

Any fuel, including the wood used in this stove, can produce carbon monoxide.

combustion   burning
fuel   any material that can be burned to produce useful energy or heat

Slow reactions with oxygen

When a substance reacts with oxygen slowly, it is called slow oxidation. We have all seen the results of slow oxidation. Slow oxidation causes the rusting of iron and steel in cars, bicycles, and bridges. The rust that forms on iron is the **compound** iron oxide.

Other metals also combine with oxygen slowly. The shiny surface of aluminum becomes dull grey as the aluminum combines with oxygen in air. This forms a coating of aluminum oxide on the metal.

Reduction

Reduction is the opposite of oxidation. Reduction reactions remove oxygen from a substance. These reactions are often used to remove oxygen from a metal **oxide** to get a useful metal, such as zinc.

Rusty rocks

Some rocks contain **minerals** with iron in them. If these rocks are exposed to the air, they will react with the oxygen in the air. The rocks then become colored red or orange, just like rust. Even a tiny amount of iron in a rock can combine with oxygen to form reddish iron oxide.

This roaring forest fire is an example of combustion. Flames, smoke, and tremendous heat result from this **chemical reaction.**

oxidation   reaction in which a substance joins with oxygen
reduction   removing oxygen from an oxide

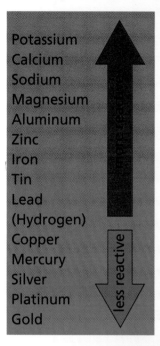

Potassium
Calcium
Sodium
Magnesium
Aluminum
Zinc
Iron
Tin
Lead
(Hydrogen)
Copper
Mercury
Silver
Platinum
Gold

more reactive

less reactive

Metals and water

Most common metals do not react with the **compound** water. However, metals such as lithium, sodium, potassium, rubidium, and cesium react violently with water. Calcium, strontium, and barium react with cold water. But they react more slowly than metals like lithium. Magnesium reacts very slowly with cold water. The reaction between a metal and water produces a compound called a **hydroxide** and hydrogen gas.

Metals and acids

Some metals react with **acids** while others do not. The **activity series** chart tells us which metals react with acids. Any metal listed above hydrogen will react with an acid to produce hydrogen gas. The metal **displaces** the hydrogen in the acid. Any metal below hydrogen in the chart will not react with an acid to produce hydrogen gas.

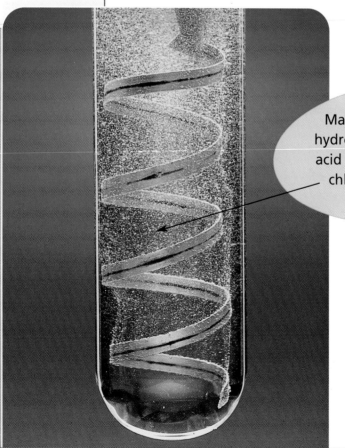

Magnesium displaces the hydrogen from hydrochloric acid to produce magnesium chloride and bubbles of hydrogen gas.

Fast Fact
When a metal reacts with acid, the test tube gets warm because the reaction is exothermic.

hydroxide   compound of a metal and a hydrogen-oxygen group

Metals and other compounds

In a **chemical reaction**, some metals will displace other metals in a compound. For example, when iron reacts with copper sulfate, the iron displaces the copper to form iron sulfate. Pure copper is also produced. The reactivity series can be used to predict which metals will displace any metal in compounds. A metal will displace any metal below it in the chart. For example, magnesium will displace lead from the compound lead chloride. This produces magnesium chloride and lead. The reaction happens because magnesium is above lead in the chart. But lead will not displace aluminum from the compound aluminum chloride. This is because lead is below aluminum in the chart.

Some metals, such as this potassium, react violently with water. Because of this, they must be stored in mineral oil or paraffin.

Mending tracks

When aluminum reacts with iron oxide, the **products** are aluminum oxide and iron. So much heat is produced during this **displacement reaction** that the iron melts. A pot containing the **reactants** is placed over the spot where two sections of railway track meet. The melted iron flows into the gap between the sections and welds them together.

◄ ◄ ◄ ◄ ◄ ◄ ◄ ◄ ◄ ◄
Look back at page 20 to find out how displacement reactions work.

Runaway train

In 1996 a runaway train derailed in the town of Leadville, Colorado. Two tanker cars carrying sulfuric acid smashed open. The acid poured across a highway. Almost 2 million pounds (900,000 kilograms) of soda ash (sodium oxide) and **lime** (calcium oxide) were needed to neutralize the spill.

Neutralization reactions

An **acid** will react with a **base**. A base is a substance that will react with acids and neutralize them. Metal **hydroxides** and metal **oxides** form bases when they dissolve in water. The reaction between an acid and a base forms a **neutral** substance. A neutral substance is neither an acid nor a base. Water is a neutral substance. The reaction between an acid and a base is called **neutralization.** In a neutralization reaction, an acid and a base react to form water and a **salt,** as shown below.

acid	+	base	→	water	+	salt
hydrochloric acid	+	sodium hydroxide	→	water	+	sodium chloride
HCl	+	NaOH	→	H_2O	+	NaCl

In this reaction, the hydrogen from the acid switches places with the sodium from the base. The hydrogen and hydroxide join to form water, or H_2O. The salt produced is sodium chloride.

Special suits protect people who clean up acid spills.

carbonate   compound of carbon, oxygen, and another element

Salts

Sodium chloride is the **compound** we commonly call salt. Sodium chloride is used for making ice cream, dyes, rubber, soap, and many other items. But it is just one of many different salts. A salt is a compound that is produced when an acid reacts with a base. The reaction between sulfuric acid and potassium hydroxide produces the salt potassium sulfate. Potassium sulfate is used in fertilizers to make plants grow better. The reaction between nitric acid and potassium hydroxide produces the salt potassium nitrate. This salt is used to stop foods from rotting. It is also used to make fertilizers and explosives.

Other acid reactions

Acids also react with compounds called **hydrogen carbonates** and **carbonates**. Limestone is calcium carbonate. Acids react with carbonates to produce a calcium salt and bubbles of carbon dioxide gas.

Trucks that carry **hazardous** materials must be labeled. Cards showing the identification number of the chemical and possible dangers are placed on the sides and ends of tankers. This tanker is carrying sulfuric acid.

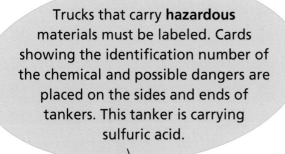

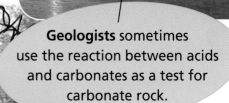

Geologists sometimes use the reaction between acids and carbonates as a test for carbonate rock.

neutralization   reaction between an acid and a base to form water and a salt

Reactions in Nature

Chemosynthesis

Sunlight cannot reach the deep parts of the ocean. **Bacteria** that live there make food by a process called **chemosynthesis**. The process takes place where hot water spurts out of the ocean floor. Bacteria make food using sulfur **compounds** found in the hot water. The bacteria are then eaten by crabs and tube worms.

Tube worms eat bacteria that live without sunlight.

◀◀◀◀◀◀◀◀◀◀ Turn back to page 23 to find out what endothermic reactions are.

Eucalyptus trees make their own food using photosynthesis. The koala eats the leaves. It then uses respiration to get energy from the leaves it has eaten.

Word Bank   photosynthesis   chemical reaction in which carbon dioxide and water react to form glucose and oxygen

Photosynthesis

The green parts of plants, such as leaves and some stems, make food during **photosynthesis**. Sunlight shines onto a plant's leaves. The green chemical chlorophyll in the leaves traps the light **energy** from the Sun. Carbon dioxide gas is taken into the leaves through tiny openings. Water comes up from the roots of the plant and travels through tiny tubes to the stems and the leaves. When they come together, the Sun's energy powers a reaction between the water and carbon dioxide to produce a kind of sugar, called **glucose**, and oxygen gas. Photosynthesis is an **endothermic reaction**. It needs energy from light to happen. The equation for photosynthesis is shown below.

$$\text{carbon dioxide} + \text{water} \rightarrow \text{glucose} + \text{oxygen}$$
$$6CO_2 + 6H_2O \rightarrow C_6H_{12}O_6 + 6O_2$$

Respiration

All living things need energy to grow. Plants get this energy from the glucose they make. Animals get glucose by eating plants or other animals. This glucose gives them the energy they need. **Respiration** is a **chemical reaction** that happens in living things. It is the opposite of photosynthesis. During respiration, glucose and oxygen react to produce carbon dioxide and water. Respiration is an **exothermic reaction**. It gives off energy that living things need. The equation for respiration is shown below.

$$\text{glucose} + \text{oxygen} \rightarrow \text{carbon dioxide} + \text{water}$$
$$C_6H_{12}O_6 + 6O_2 \rightarrow 6CO_2 + 6H_2O$$

Fast Fact
Plants also respire. They use the glucose they made during photosynthesis.

Digesting food

Iodine is used as a test for starch. If starch is present, a chemical reaction between the iodine and starch produces a dark-colored substance.

Starch is a compound found in foods like bread, made of simple sugar units joined together. In the body, a chemical in **saliva** begins to break down starch into sugar. If a person chews on a piece of bread for a minute, it will start to taste sweet. That is because a chemical reaction has changed the starch to sugar.

Lechuguilla Cave

Lechuguilla Cave in New Mexico did not form the way most caves do. It formed when hydrogen sulfide gas seeped up through deep cracks in the earth. A **chemical reaction** between the hydrogen sulfide and oxygen in the **groundwater** formed sulfuric acid.

Sulfuric acid ate through layers of limestone underground. It left a maze of tunnels and caves.

Cave formation

Acids react with **carbonates** to produce a **salt**, water, and carbon dioxide gas. For example, hydrochloric acid reacts with calcium carbonate to form the salt calcium chloride, water, and carbon dioxide. Caves form because of the reaction of an acid with carbonate rocks.

The formation of caves starts with rain. Rainwater joins with carbon dioxide gas in the air. This **synthesis reaction** forms a weak acid called carbonic acid.

The acid seeps through cracks in the ground and reacts with calcium carbonate rocks like limestone. This reaction **dissolves** the limestone. It forms the salt calcium hydrogen carbonate, water, and carbon dioxide. Caves and tunnels form as the acid moves through the rock. After thousands of years, huge underground rooms and tunnels can form.

Fast Fact

Soda pops are fizzy because they contain bubbles of carbon dioxide gas. Some of this dissolves in the drink and forms carbonic acid, which is bad for teeth.

fossil fuel   oil, coal, and gas found in the earth's crust, formed from ancient plants and animals

Acid rain

The burning of **fossil fuels** causes acid rain. It releases sulfur dioxide and nitrogen oxides into the air. These compounds react with **water vapor** in the air to form sulfuric acid and nitric acid. These acids then fall to the earth in rain and snow.

Many parts of the United States, Canada, and Europe have been affected by acid rain. Acid rain dissolves marble and limestone in buildings and statues. Marble and limestone are carbonate rocks. It also kills some types of tree. Water in some lakes is so acidic that all life in them has been destroyed. It also makes soils acidic, so some plants cannot grow in them.

Neutralizing acidic lakes

Many plants and animals cannot live in acidic water. So countries like Norway treat waters that have been damaged by acid rain. Powdered limestone is spread on the surface of lakes. The limestone **neutralizes** the acid in the water.

The chemical reaction between carbonic acid and carbonate rocks forms the shapes on cave walls.

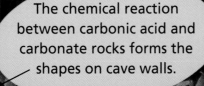

Airplanes, helicopters, and boats are used to spread lime on acidic lakes. Plants and animals can live in the water once the acid is neutralized.

groundwater   water that soaks into the ground and collects in tiny spaces between pieces of rock and soil

Amazing Reactions

Nonstick cookware

In the 1930s scientists were testing a gas they hoped could be used to cool refrigerators. They stored containers of the gas on dry ice. Later, they opened the containers and discovered the gas had disappeared. A chemical reaction had produced a slippery, white powder that coated the insides of the canisters.

This slippery substance, discovered by an accidental chemical reaction, is now used to coat the inside of pots and pans. The coated pans keep food from sticking.

Baking

Yeasts are tiny living things that you can only see with a microscope. People mix yeast into bread dough. Yeast reacts with the sugars in wheat flour. The reaction forms carbon dioxide gas and alcohol. The gas creates thousands of little bubbles that cause the bread dough to **expand** or rise. The heat from baking drives off the carbon dioxide and the alcohol. But tiny holes are left throughout the bread where the carbon dioxide bubbles were.

Other breads, such as soda bread, do not use yeast to make dough rise. Instead they use baking soda (sodium bicarbonate). For baking soda to produce carbon dioxide, it must react with an **acid.** Sour milk or buttermilk that contains lactic acid is often used.

These tiny yeast cells can only be seen under a microscope. A reaction between yeast and flour makes bread rise.

digestion   breakdown of food so it can be used by the body

Body enzymes

We need food for our bodies to grow and repair themselves. The food we eat must be broken down so our bodies can use it. **Digestion** is the process of breaking down chemicals in food into a form that the body can use. Special substances, called **enzymes**, **catalyze** digestion by speeding up the **chemical reactions** that break down food. Digestion is a series of different chemical reactions that start in the mouth.

When food reaches the stomach, enzymes start to break down proteins from foods like meat, fish, and milk. But most digestion happens after food leaves the stomach and goes into the intestines. Many enzymes are released into the small intestine. When digestion is complete, food materials are in a thin, watery form that the body can use.

◄ ◄ ◄ ◄ ◄ ◄ ◄ ◄ ◄ ◄ ◄

Turn back to page 35 to find out how digestion starts in your mouth.

Lactose intolerance

The enzyme lactase breaks down sugar in milk. It is present in the intestines of normal human babies and most adults of European descent. But people from Africa and Asia and their older children often lack this enzyme. So do most Australian Aborigines and Native Americans. This condition is known as lactose intolerance.

People with lactose intolerance do not have the enzyme to digest milk and milk products such as cheese, sour cream, and ice cream. Symptoms of lactose intolerance include cramps and diarrhea.

expand   become larger in size; take up more space

Reactions in your mouth

Bacteria that live in human mouths produce **acids.** The acids react with chemicals in teeth and eat away the outer covering of teeth, the enamel. Then the bacteria and acids start to attack the inside of teeth. This can lead to painful **cavities.**

Using hand warmers

People who go outdoors in cold weather sometimes put hand warmers inside their gloves. Hand warmers are small pouches that come sealed in a package. You have to open the package and shake the pouch to mix the chemicals in it with the air. Chemical hand warmers work because iron powder in the pouch reacts with oxygen in the air to form rust. Salt and powdered charcoal in the pouch act as **catalysts.** They speed up this **exothermic reaction.** This means heat is given off at a faster rate than with normal rusting. Some hand warmers can stay at about 135 °F (57 °C) for up to 12 hours.

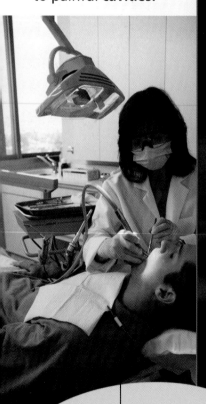

Fast Fact
The same **chemical reactions** are used in heat wraps that people use on their backs or necks to treat pain.

The chemical reaction in a lightstick releases energy in the form of light.

It is important to brush teeth and see a dentist often to keep teeth free of acid-producing bacteria.

Using lightsticks

Lightsticks are used by campers and scuba divers, and for decoration and fun. A lightstick is a plastic tube with a small glass container inside it. When you bend the plastic tube, the glass container breaks. This lets chemicals that were inside the glass mix with the chemicals in the plastic tube. Once these chemicals touch each other, a reaction starts to happen. The reaction produces light, causing the stick to glow. This is an exothermic reaction because light **energy** is given off.

If you put a lightstick in a cold place, the reaction will slow down. Less light will be produced, but the lightstick will glow for a longer time. If you put the lightstick in hot water, the reaction will speed up. The stick will glow more brightly, but it will not last as long.

Hard water

The hardness of water is a measure of the amount of calcium and magnesium **dissolved** in it. These **salts** react with chemicals in soap to form a **precipitate** called soap scum. Soap scum sticks to the sides of baths and sinks.

Some people use water softeners in their homes. Chemical reactions in the softeners make the water soft.

THE SOFT SOLUTION TO HARD WATER
SALT FOR WATER SOFTENERS
25kg

D   REGENERIERSALZ
F   SEL POUR ADOUCISSEURS D'EAU   B
NL   ZOUT VOOR WATERVERZACHTERS
     SALE PER ADDOLCIMENTO ACQUA
S   SALT FOR VATTENAVHÅRDNING
DK   SALT TIL BLØDGØRING
N   SALT FOR BLØ...RING

◄ ◄ ◄ ◄ ◄ ◄ ◄ ◄ ◄ ◄ ◄
Turn back to page 12 to find out what a precipitate is.

Daily blood tests

People who have diabetes must check their blood glucose levels several times a day. A number of different kinds of testing devices can be used. But they all depend on reactions between the glucose in a person's blood and other chemicals.

Medical science

Doctors use blood chemical tests to find out if a person has certain diseases. The tests measure chemicals in the blood to find out how body **organs** are working. One common test measures how much **glucose** is in the blood. A high glucose level tells the doctor a person might have **diabetes.** Other tests measure waste products that healthy kidneys filter out. High levels of these products mean a person's kidneys are not working properly. Measuring **enzymes** made by the liver tells a doctor if a person has liver disease. A doctor can have many other tests done to check a person's health. All these tests depend on **chemical reactions** between chemicals in a person's blood and other chemicals that are added to a sample of the blood.

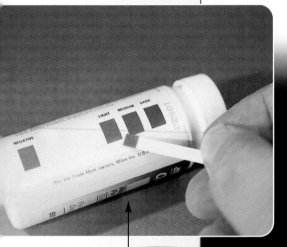

Some glucose tests show different colors on a test strip. The color the strip turns tells the person what his or her glucose level is.

organ   body part such as a heart, lung, liver, or kidney

Forensic science

Police also use chemical tests to help solve crimes. Luminol is a chemical that police use to look for traces of blood at a crime scene. Police mix a powder form of Luminol with hydrogen peroxide. They spray this **mixture** where they think there might be blood. Then the lights are turned out. A very slow **exothermic reaction** happens between the Luminol and the peroxide. A faint blue-green glow is eventually seen. But a **catalyst** speeds up the reaction and the glow will be seen much faster. It will also be much brighter. One catalyst of this reaction is iron. Iron is found in human blood. So if blood is present, police will see a bright glow in just a few seconds.

Take a deep breath and blow

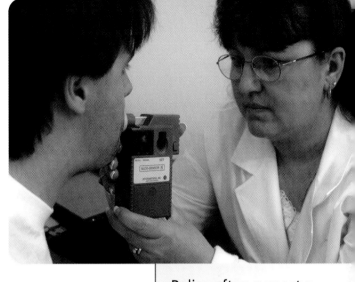

Police often suspect a person who is driving dangerously of being drunk. In the past they used a blow-in-the-bag breathalyzer, which contained a red-orange chemical. The red-orange chemical reacted with alcohol in a person's breath. If it turned green, the person had been drinking.

Luminol will glow even if the traces of blood are many years old. It works even if the area has been cleaned.

Further Information

Organizations

Science Made Simple

Learn about science "hands on." Site includes science news, projects, facts, more. **sciencemadesimple.com**

Rader Studios

Fun science news, plus activities including quizzes, experiments, tutorials, and more. **chem4kids.com**

Lawrence Livermore National Laboratory

Get science news from a national security laboratory. **llnl.gov**

Books

Fullick, Ann. *Chemicals in Action*. Chicago: Heinemann, 2000.

Fullick, Ann. *Matter*. Chicago: Heinemann, 1999.

Snedden, Robert. *Material World: Changing Materials*. Chicago: Heinemann, 2001.

World Wide Web

If you want to find out more about **chemical reactions,** you can search the Internet using keywords like these:

- fireworks
- "chemical tests"
- chemicals + reactions + displacement
- "neutralization reactions"
- rusting + iron
- crime + science
- reactions + catalysts

You can also find your own keywords by using headings or words from this book. Use the search tips opposite to help you find the most useful websites.

Search tips

There are billions of pages on the Internet so it can be difficult to find exactly what you are looking for. For example, if you just type in "water" on a search engine like Google, you will get a list of 85 million web pages. These search skills will help you find useful websites more quickly:

- Know exactly what you want to find out about first.
- Use simple keywords instead of whole sentences.
- Use two to six keywords in a search, putting the most important words first.
- Be precise—only use names of people, places, or things.
- If you want to find words that go together, put quote marks around them, for example "chemical reaction."
- Use the advanced section of your search engine.
- Use the + sign to add certain words to your search.

Where to search

Search engine

A search engine looks through the entire web and lists all the sites that match the words in the search box. It can give thousands of links, but the best matches are at the top of the list, on the first page. Try **google.com.**

Search directory

A search directory is more like a library of websites that have been sorted by a person instead of a computer. You can search by keyword or subject and browse through the different sites in the same way you would look through books on a library shelf. A good example is **yahooligans.com.**

Glossary

acid compound that contains hydrogen and has a pH of less than 7

acid rain low-pH rain produced when pollutants react with water in the air

activity series list of materials ordered by how easily they react with acids

atom smallest particle of an element

bacteria living things so small they can only be seen with a microscope

base compound with pH more than 7

carbonate compound of carbon, oxygen, and another element

catalyst substance that speeds up a reaction without being changed itself

cavity hole in a tooth

chemical property feature that tells how a substance will react

chemical reaction change that produces one or more new substances

chemical symbol short way of writing the name of an element

chemosynthesis chemical reaction that happens in the deep ocean where sunlight does not reach, in which bacteria make food from sulfur compounds

combustion burning

compost mixture of rotting plant material

compound substance made of two or more elements joined together chemically

concentration amount of a substance in a certain volume

corrode to be damaged by a chemical reaction

decomposition reaction chemical reaction in which a compound breaks apart into simpler substances

diabetes condition in which there is too much glucose in the blood

digestion breakdown of food so it can be used by the body

displace to take the place of something

displacement reaction chemical reaction in which one or more elements in a compound displace another element

dissolve break down into molecules and mix evenly and completely

electrolysis using electricity to break a compound apart

element substance made of only one kind of atom

endothermic reaction reaction that needs energy

energy ability to cause change

enzyme chemical that speeds up reactions in living things

exothermic reaction reaction that gives off energy, usually in the form of heat or light

expand to become larger in size; to take up more space

formula symbols and numbers used to show how atoms are joined

fossil fuel oil, coal, and gas, found in the earth's crust. It was formed from ancient plants and animals.

fuel any material that can be burned to produce useful energy or heat

geologist scientist who studies rocks

glucose compound that is a form of sugar

groundwater water that soaks into the ground and collects in tiny spaces between pieces of rock and soil

hazardous dangerous or harmful

hydrogen carbonate compound of a metal and a hydrogen-carbon-oxygen group

hydroxide compound of a metal and a hydrogen-oxygen group

inhibitor substance that slows down a chemical reaction

lime common name for calcium oxide

mass amount of matter in an object; measured in ounces or pounds (grams or kilograms)

matter anything that takes up space and has mass

mineral nonliving solid material

mixture material made from elements or compounds not joined chemically

molecule two or more atoms held together by chemical bonds

neutral neither an acid nor a basic

neutralization reaction between an acid and a base to form water and a salt

odorless having no smell

organ body part such as a heart, lung, liver, or kidney

oxidation reaction in which a substance joins with oxygen

oxide compound of oxygen and another element

particle tiny piece

photosynthesis chemical reaction in which carbon dioxide and water react to form glucose and oxygen

physical change change in how something looks, but not in what makes it up

physical property feature that can be seen or measured without changing what the substance is made of

pollute to add harmful substances to air, water, or land

precipitate solid compound, produced in a chemical reaction, that does not dissolve

product substance formed by a chemical reaction

property feature of something

reactant substance that reacts with another substance during a chemical reaction

reaction rate measure of how fast a chemical reaction happens

reduction removing oxygen from an oxide

respiration chemical reaction in which glucose and oxygen react to form carbon dioxide and water

saliva watery liquid that keeps the mouth moist and helps digest starch in food

salt compound formed when an acid reacts with a base

starch compound made of simple sugar units joined together

state of matter whether something is solid, liquid, or gas

surface area amount of a substance in contact with a reactant

symbol equation way of describing a chemical reaction using chemical formulas

synthesis reaction chemical reaction in which two or more elements or compounds join to form one compound

tarnish to become dull by a reaction with air

water vapor water in gas form

Index